W9-AOM-145

PEN IN HAND

Pen in Hand

A SIMPLIFIED GUIDE TO
"INSTANT" HANDWRITING ANALYSIS

FLORRY NADALL

DOUBLEDAY & COMPANY, INC.
Garden City, New York

ACKNOWLEDGMENTS

I wish to express my sincerest thanks to the many people who have contributed their handwriting and photographs for use in the illustrations of this volume.

My gratitude also goes to the officials of the Federal and Commonwealth governments in Puerto Rico whom I have met during my many years of association with the Caribe Hilton Hotel. Their aid has been invaluable in obtaining illustrations of great interest.

And I am especially appreciative of the assistance Joel Magruder has rendered in preparing the textual portions of the book.

Lastly, I am deeply indebted to Mr. Robert E. Banker for the encouragement and faith I received from him, which prompted me to write this book.

Library of Congress Catalog Card Number: 65-22589

Printed in the United States of America

Designed by Freda Browne

First Edition

TO MY FATHER

A man of principle and honor,
who never despaired, even
in the presence of the
final adversity

CONTENTS

Part III INSTANT CHARACTER AND APTITUDE GUIDE

ILLUSTRATIONS OF HANDWRITING OF PEOPLE OF OUR TIME

Samples of Handwriting of People with Physical or Mental Disorder

Samples of Handwriting of People Convicted of Crimes

"THE PORTRAIT OF YOURSELF"

Your handwriting is a reflection of your personality. From the depths of the mind an impulse flows to a hand that sets a pen upon the paper and moves it, in delicate tracings, across the surface. The writing born of this impulse tells many tales beyond the limits of mere words. For the pen and hand are subtle servants of the mind, and reveal the very nature of their master. The lines and curves of every man's writing are a portrait of his inner self.

INTRODUCTION

Getting to know people as they really are: this was the interest, inspired by childhood curiosity, which guided me to the captivating and most informative study of graphology.

When I was a little girl, living in Vienna and Hamburg, I was always fascinated by people, and the relation that their voices, gestures, and dress bore to their inner selves. While riding on streetcars, I enjoyed listening to the voices of people seated behind me, engaged in conversation. I would try to construct in my mind a picture of them, basing my guesses on the tone of voice, accent, and choice of words. Then I would turn my head to look at the people out of the corner of my eye, to see how close I had reproduced in my mind the real person that sat there. Sometimes my guess would be surprisingly accurate; at other times, the person's appearance would be entirely different from the image I had formed. Often I would wonder if there might not be a more reliable way to probe beneath the surface of people I would meet—some gesture, perhaps, that would be a little window into their inner character.

It was during this period of my life that I first heard of graphology, or handwriting analysis. From the start, it seemed to me that this might be that "window" that I had been seeking. With youthful enthusiasm, I began to read everything on the subject that I could find; and the results were most gratifying. Graphology provided such a faithful source of information about the character and the capabilities of people that it became a lifelong interest for me.

Graphology, I learned, was no mere guessing game, as had been my streetcar pastimes. As early as 1843, the French churchman Abbe Flandrin had introduced a very thorough study of the science, which later stirred a considerable interest in Europe. Inquiries and studies were produced in increasing number throughout the later years of the last century, so that by the second decade of the present century, graphology was recognized as a scientific method of analysis, governed by generally accepted rules.

Today, large corporations, police courts, physicians, and psychiatrists benefit from the use of this science in aptitude tests, in tabulation of mental stability, and in the authentication of documents.

Two of the more eminent authorities in graphology with whom I have been privileged to study are Dr. Oscar Meyer and De Witt Lucas.

Dr. Meyer, a former European attorney, has a wide variety of studies which today are regarded as excellent contributions to the literature of the science. On the West Coast, De Witt Lucas has made notable accomplishments in the fields of criminology and legal research.

Graphology has been my own profession, leading to stimulating activities in both the business and entertainment worlds, for over twenty years. During my travels to different parts of the world, I have had the opportunity to analyze handwriting for many guests of Hilton hotels, with whom I have been long associated, as well as an inestimable number of other people from all corners of the world and all walks of life. The handwriting and photographs of some of the many celebrities I have met in the course of my travels are included in this book.

I have also had the opportunity frequently to collaborate with business firms in the personnel selection, by analyzing the handwriting of prospective employees under consideration for posts ranging from the highest executive levels down through the ranks.

My own experiences in these past two decades demonstrate that graphology is a most useful means of probing deeply into a person's nature—his character, his emotions, his sincerity, and his capability. The value of having at hand a ready gauge of these qualities, in educational, business, and social contacts, is obvious.

It is for those people who would like to know more about themselves, their friends, associates, and even their children, that I have written this book. I have designed it so that, at a glance, anyone can pick out the meaningful aspects of a handwriting and know their significance.

This book is also written for the many people whom I have enjoyed meeting in my career, who have asked me someday to set down the basic principles of graphology in a simple form.

Finally, I would like to say that I hope you, too, find interesting and rewarding my humble contribution to the fascinating and entertaining science that has so engrossed my attention.

Florry Nadall

PART I

BASIC FEATURES

Basic features of handwriting are like the first outline in the painting of a portrait: in a swift, general way, they capture the fundamental characteristics of a person.

HOW TO ANALYZE A HANDWRITING SAMPLE

Significant Factors to Consider

Although there are millions of people in the world, no two can be found who write exactly alike. Children taught to write in one classroom in the same basic way, after a few years will develop their own individual style of writing. This fact is a consequence of the infinite variety of human character, personality, and ability. Since handwriting reflects the individual variations of these traits, no two handwritings will be precisely alike.

Your impression of a person is influenced subconsciously by the appearance of his handwriting. You associate a simple, legible specimen of writing with a modest, dependable, and stable person, just as you would expect a bold, heavy writing from a dynamic, determined individual. By the same token, a lavishly flourished style of writing with ornamental capitals would be natural for a pretentious or eccentric personality. And an irregular, illegible, rangy scrawl of writing is expressive of an inconsistent, tense, and impatient type of person, although people sometimes do write irregularly when under emotional stress, or in extreme haste, or when fatigued, or ailing.

You have probably seen many examples similar to these following styles of writing:

1. Simple, legible handwriting — *simple, legible*
2. Bold, heavy handwriting — *bold heavy*
3. Lavishly flourished handwriting — *flourished*
4. Illegible, irregular handwriting — [illegible]

These four samples of handwriting styles serve to illustrate that you can form a general impression of the nature of the writer from no more than a momentary study of the over-all appearance of the script.

Getting the general impression of the handwriting specimen you wish to analyze is a very important first step toward a more complete understanding of the writer's character and aptitudes. Always pause before beginning an analysis, and give yourself time to form this impression. The things you discover later, when you look into the meaning of the details of the handwriting, will modify and enlarge upon this original opinion.

There are two ways you can use this book. If you wish to construct a complete analysis of a writer's character traits, you should check the writing sample's details with each chapter in Parts I and II.

But if you are hurried and wish only to know about one specific ability, character drawback, or possible illness sign, turn to Part III—the INSTANT APTITUDE GUIDE. To use this final section, simply check the writing sample against the signs in the boxes which appear there.

To establish a reliable, complete, and detailed analysis, you should obtain a handwriting specimen of about eight lines (or fifty words) and a signature. It should be written in ink, preferably not with a ballpoint pen, and never with a pencil, on a letter-sized sheet of unruled paper.

Do not attempt to analyze short notes and memos which are usually hurriedly scrawled. Postal cards are particularly unsuitable for an analysis, because of the limited writing space.

If the writer is not present at the time of analysis, it would be wise to obtain his approximate age, since his handwriting will reveal emotional maturity, rather than chronological age. It would also be advisable to be informed about the sex of the writer, since a handwriting specimen may show characteristics common to both sexes. To cite a case, the handwriting of a hard-driving business woman may contain signs of masculine qualities and display a degree of aggressiveness unusual in a woman.

It would be helpful to know if the writer is left-handed, in order to better determine the meaning of his writing slant. The meaning of a left-handed writer's slant is the reverse of that of a right-handed writer, as is explained in Chapter 2 of Part I.

Of all the words a person writes, the signature is the one most significant combination of letters. It is the group of letters most frequently written together, and since it is a highly emphatic written gesture of a person's ego, it may be called his written calling card, designed to symbolize that person in the eyes of others. It presents his outer personality.

The signature should receive a good deal of attention.

But it should never be taken as the only basis for a reliable analysis. It should be considered along with a person's general handwriting.

General writing covers the vast majority of writing that people do. It is the everyday writing of letters and reports, usually done without conscious attention, that reveals the true disposition of the writer. It presents his innate character, often concealed from others.

A final preliminary word of caution: For the sake of accuracy and fairness, you should resist the temptation to make snap judgments on the basis of an occasional letter formation in a handwriting specimen. A slip of the hand or a bad pen can cause variations from usual writing habits. A person's state of mind or health, at the time of writing, can also cause temporary changes in some aspects of his handwriting, but may not have any lasting effects on his personality. These conditions should certainly be kept in mind when assessing a person's character and aptitudes. It would also be helpful to have specimens written on different occasions by the same person, if possible, so that momentary variations might be spotted and not be given undue importance.

It should be remembered that a character trait will show up in many ways, in many different aspects of a person's handwriting. You can be certain that you have hit upon the correct traits when they appear repeatedly in many of the writing formations discussed in the pages that follow.

The Hon. John F. Kennedy,
late President of the United States
of America.

Mrs. Jacqueline Kennedy

THE WHITE HOUSE
WASHINGTON

With the best wishes
John F. Kennedy

Jacqueline Kennedy

(These handwriting samples, consisting of only a few words, are adequate for merely a brief personality sketch.)

The late President Kennedy's handwriting showed him to be an energetic, enterprising, and resolute man. The heavy pen pressure of his writing, together with the strong final downstrokes, and the omitted initial strokes, expressed his extraordinary intensity and decisiveness.

Mrs. Jacqueline Kennedy's handwriting, with graceful, printed capitals, and disconnected letters within the words, reveals that she is a versatile woman, with a high degree of creativeness and originality. The slightly backward slant in her signature expresses reserve and self-control.

Chapter 1

BASE LINE

The Degree of Stability, Optimism, Ambition

The base line of a person's handwriting is one of the most clearly visible signs that a writing sample can provide. The base line is the course followed by the bottom of the letters in each line of writing—excluding the lower loops and strokes on letters such as "g" and "p". It expresses the range of emotions, from optimism to depression. It also shows whether the writer is logical and responsible, or flighty and unreliable.

To plot a writer's base line, in order to see it in the clearest fashion, trace a line lightly along the lower edge of each letter, in a continuous line across the page. Some base lines, you will notice, are nearly straight. Others will wave up and down within the same line of writing. Still others will rise gradually and steadily from left to right, while some will just as steadily head downward.

You should remember that a highly emotional person's writing may show changes in the base line, as he changes in mood. One day it may rise across the page, only to shift and angle off downward the following day. The more stable person will show, in contrast, little variation in the base line of his writing, which will tend to be fairly straight.

By glancing at the base lines of a handwritten message, you can determine the prevailing emotional state of the writer, even before reading the words his message contains.

BASE LINE (Straight, Upward, Downward)

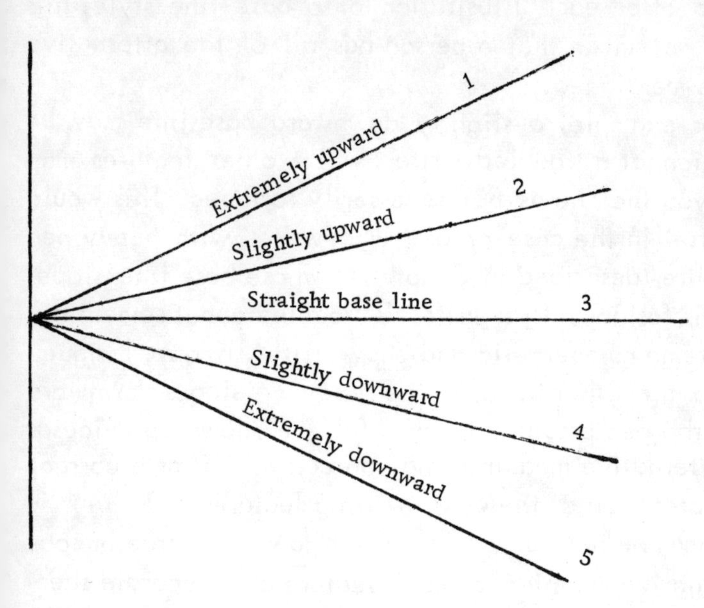

BASE LINE

	Sample	
1. Extremely upward	extremely upward	Imaginative, eccentric, enthusiastic, exuberant
2. Slightly upward	slightly upward	Spontaneous, confident, optimistic, ambitious
3. Straight (or nearly)	almost straight	Dependable, consistent, logical, self-assured
4. Slightly downward	slightly downward	Indecisive, troubled, discontented, fatigued
5. Extremely downward	Extremely downward	Pessimistic, ailing, despondent, apathetic
6. Irregular, changeable	Irregular	Unstable, tense, careless, moody

Although there are several possible character traits listed after each illustration of a base-line style, this does not mean that a person has all of the alternative traits mentioned.

For example, a slightly downward base line may be the sign of a troubled writer, while other features may tell you that he is not necessarily fatigued. This would be true in the case of one who writes with heavy pen pressure (described in Chapter 4) whose base line slopes in this fashion. This writer is troubled about something, but remains energetic and shows little, if any, fatigue.

On the other hand, if the base line slopes downward and the pen pressure is thin, fatigue shows up twice as an alternative meaning, and you can take it as a correct interpretation of these two writing features.

It may be helpful for you to jot down the three or four alternative meanings of each feature on a separate sheet of paper as you proceed through the chapters. As your list grows, you will notice some traits appearing more frequently than others. These often-repeated character traits will be the ones you are looking for, since the facets of a person's inner make-up show through consistently in many different parts of his handwriting.

■

Yo nací en
Baní República
Dominicana en
el día 1?0 1

This alarming handwriting belongs to a young twenty-one-year-old girl just released from a mental hospital. The marked downward slant of the base line is a warning sign of suicidal tendencies and mental disorder. The long initial strokes are signs of resentment, and also indicate that the girl lives bound by her past experiences.

■

Piedras, Puerto
Rico. Mis
Padres están
muertos.

The handwriting of this thirty-three-year-old woman shows a mental struggle. The uneven slant and jagged base line reveal a mind that has been unbalanced by inner conflicts and disturbances. The big loops of the letter "d" (in "Piedras" and "padres") and those in the letter "t" (in "estan" and "muertos") are signs of an oversensitive nature. The heavy pen pressure serves to emphasize the strength of the deep-felt emotions.

The Hon. Robert F. Wagner, Mayor of New York City.

I am enclosing
my photograph as
you suggested.

Robert F. Wagner

The firm, heavy writing of the Hon. Robert F. Wagner, the popular administrator and political figure, reveal that he is a man of determination and independence. Diplomacy is evident in the closed letters "o" and "a". The even spacing between the lines and words are signs of excellent reasoning power and stability.

Chapter 2

SLANT

The Degree of Emotion, Reason, Enterprise

Slant—the direction in which letters angle up from the line of writing—indicates the relative power of emotional drives. Forward slant expresses an emotional, possibly impulsive nature. A writer whose slant is forward-leaning is ruled by his feelings rather than by reason. The person whose writing is vertical, or slants backward, may also have deep emotions; but his reason will always dominate his impulses.

The slant of the signature reveals the outer personality, that face which is shown to others. The general writing, the everyday writing of letters and reports, expresses the inner feelings, the innate character, often hidden from others.

The slant of a signature may differ from that of the general handwriting. For instance, the signature may slant forward, while the general writing leans backward. This reveals that the response shown toward others differs from the inner feelings of the writer.

If the signature and general writing slant in the same direction, there is no divergence displayed between the inner and outer sentiments.

A slant so extreme that the writing falls forward almost to the base line, coupled with heavy, muddy writing, indicates a suicidal tendency.

SLANT Forward, Backward, Straight

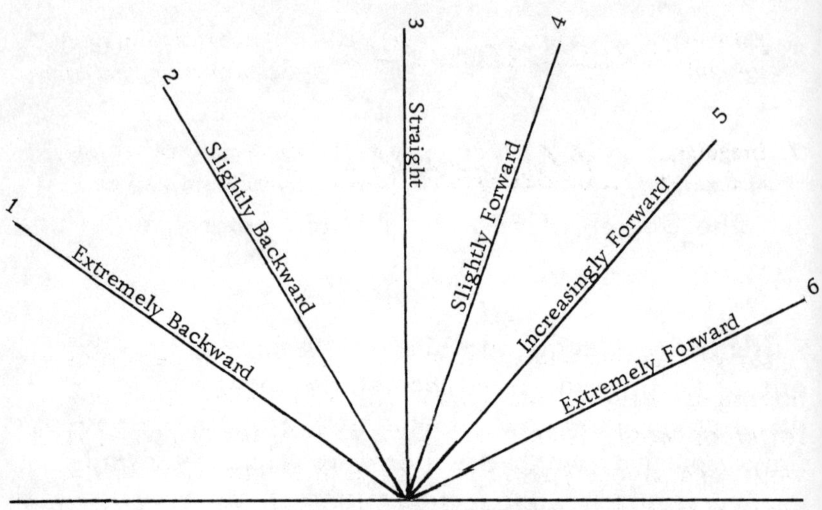

BASE LINE OF WRITING

This diagram is designed for right-handed people. For left-handed people, it should be used in reverse. For example: if a left-handed person writes with a slant that looks like No. 6, it should be treated as No. 1.

SLANT

1. Extremely backward	Extremely backward	Mind-ruled, inhibited egotistical, arrogant
2. Slightly backward	Slightly backward	Mind-ruled, reserved, controlled, critical
3. Straight	Straight no slant	Self-assured, reserved, logical, discriminating
4. Slightly forward	Slight.ly forward	Determined, assured, enterprising, spontaneous

5. Increasingly forward	Increasingly	Emotional, impulsive, emphatic, kindhearted
6. Extremely forward	Extremely	Opinionated, irritable, argumentative, excitable
7. Irregular, changeable	Changeable	Unpredictable, moody, inconsistent, unstable

Do not be in such a hurry that you label a person as having a certain trait just because it shows up in one letter or word. Take your time and see, for example, if what one slant-type tells you is also apparent fairly consistently in the rest of the writing sample.

Also remember that not all four characteristics listed after each illustration need apply to the same writer. A person who writes with a "straight" script, to cite one case, may be self-assured, but not too reserved. You may notice that while his writing is straight, he makes his capital letters large and flourished.

This type of capital modifies the interpretation of his writing slant. In this case, he may be a self-assured person, but his vanity or eccentricity—shown by the flourished capitals—may overshadow his logic and reticence and lead him to be unreasonably arrogant.

While examining slant, you should also bear in mind that a person's slant can alter within the same sample of writing. Such changes show a change of mood as he writes. You will probably notice this phenomenon in your own letter writing to a friend. You may start straight or with little slant, feeling objective and cool about what you are writing. But as you progress through the letter, you touch on some subject about which you feel deeply. Your slant may angle forward as you become more emotionally involved in what you are writing. Then, when you cool off, the slant may switch to nearly straight again.

Fairly stable people, however, will vary their writing slant only within a certain limited range—say, from straight to slightly forward. Any radical departure from this custom would be a sign of deep emotional changes within the writer.

SLANT OF SIGNATURE IN COMPARISON WITH GENERAL WRITING

General writing slant occasionally differs from signature slant.

1. Back slant in signature	Mr. Backslant	Mind-ruled, critical, controlled, reserved
Forward slant in general writing	forward slant	Responsive, emotional, impulsive, kindhearted

The back slant in this signature reveals a person that may appear to be cold and unapproachable, while the forward slant in the general writing expresses that this writer is in reality kindhearted and responsive.

2. Forward slant in signature	Mr. Forward	Responsive, emotional, impulsive, kindhearted
Back slant in general writing	back slant	Mind-ruled, critical, controlled, reserved

The forward slant in this signature expresses a kindhearted, responsive personality, while the back slant in the general writing reveals that this writer is in reality reserved and ruled by his mind.

3. Straight signature	Mr. Straight	Self-assured, reserved, discriminating, logical
Straight general writing	straight, no slant	Self-assured, reserved, discriminating, logical

This signature and general writing slant in the same direction and indicate that this writer appears outwardly exactly as he feels inwardly.

Whenever the slant of the signature and general writing is the same, no matter in what direction, the writer's outer appearance is identical with his inner feelings and nature.

■

Allow me once again to compliment
you on your extraordinary skill. I look
onward in eager anticipation to the
publishing of your book. I have already

The heavy pen pressure in the script of this eighteen-year-old young man, Robert L. Krupnick, already one of the top salesmen in the state of New York, is a clear sign of spontaneity and energy. His friendly personality is expressed in the forward-leaning slant, while the letters that reach high into the upper zone show imagination and pride. The angular formation of the letters "m", "n", "y" reveal a sharp-witted, alert mind and a daring nature.

CONRAD N. HILTON

Conrad Hilton's signature with the firm, rising "t" cross and heavy pen pressure indicates determination and will power—traits that have enabled him to rise to the position he now occupies as head of one of the world's great hotel empires. The forward slant of his handwriting shows that he is an emotionally responsive, appealing person.

(The few strokes of any signature are good for only a brief analysis.)

■

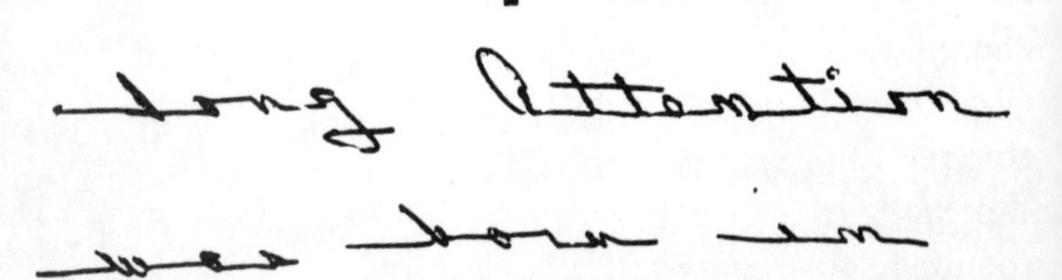

This unusual script of a seventeen-year-old girl, with a pronounced back-slant writing, angular letter formation, and long strokes running along the base line, expresses a perceptive, coolheaded and suspicious nature. The long initial and final strokes, as well as the long connecting strokes between the letters, and the closed and squeezed "o"s and "a"s reveal a critical attitude toward people and ideas.

■

8/1/63

ace ciato ciglos y medio
Los pueblos cibilizados del Antiguo
Continente tenían un conocimento
muy limitado acerca del mundo.
Creían que la tierra hera plana y
no Redonda. no se habían llegado
ha conocer la mitad de los paises del

Convicted of second-degree arson.

This writing belongs to a man confined in a penitentiary. The trembling, unbalanced writing, with the changeable slant, reveals an unpredictable nature, a mind that is almost totally unstable. The letters that stagger shakily high into the upper zone (2, 3, 4) are the mark of an imagination run wild into fantasy. The rounded, bowl-curved "t" crosses (5, 6, 7) show a drifting, weak-minded character.

Chapter 3

MARGIN

The Degree of Economy, Consistency, Tolerance

Margins govern the arrangement of writing on a sheet of paper. They are the borders of space within which a person frames his writing. They reveal the presence or absence of a creative sense of form, proportion, and beauty; the degree of economy in matters of finance; and the amount of order and consistency an individual displays in his habits of thought and conduct.

Left margins that are narrow (or nearly nonexistent) express economy and intolerance.

Left margins that are well placed (neither too narrow nor too wide) indicate a practical and consistent nature.

Wide left margins signify tolerance and originality.

Irregular margins are signs of inconsistency. If the left margin starts out narrow and widens down the page, the writer is reserved, economical, and cautious at the beginning but grows less reserved and becomes more open and generous as he proceeds.

However, if the left margin starts wide but shrinks markedly down the page, the reverse is expressed. After a rather free and unconcerned beginning, the writer grows steadily more cautious, reserved, and less liberal.

The right-hand margin is not nearly as significant as the left margin.

If the right margin is nearly similar to the left one, consistency and a sense of order is expressed.

If, however, the right margin is of a widely different width from the left margin, there is an inconsistency present in the writer's thoughts and actions.

Right margins that are much narrower than left ones are signs of someone who, once something is begun, grows more involved and less hesitant. In financial matters, this writer will tend to be more concerned about economy in the latter stages of his dealings.

A right margin far wider than the left is typical of a person who starts enterprises, then becomes hesitant before finishing them.

An extremely wide right margin is expressive of a person who is not particularly sociable, who enjoys solitude, and may possibly be indifferent toward others.

LEFT MARGIN

	Sample	
1. None	no left margin	Thrifty, narrow-minded
2. Narrow	narrow left marg	Economical, cautious
3. Average (medium)	average left marg	Practical, consistent
4. Wide	wide left marg	Liberal, tolerant
5. Irregular	Irregular left margin sometimes narrow and then wide	Inconsistent, erratic

RIGHT MARGIN

1. None	no right margin	Economical, spirited
2. Average (medium)	average margin	Practical, consistent
3. Wide	wide margin.	Impractical, reserved
4. Extremely wide	extra wide.	Indifferent, complex

Man does not write by margin alone. Neither should margin, despite its importance, be the only facet of a writing sample on which you base your analysis of his character. Remember to examine each feature of his writing in turn, as you progress through the book, and make no definite decisions as to what kind of person he is until you have probed the meaning of many quirks of his writing style.

If, for example, a person's margin habits indicate he is rather lavish, this trait will also show up in other ways. One will be the spacing between each word in a line of his writing sample. Only after you see that a trait such as this appears in several different manners, can you say that you have discovered a consistent character trait.

■

Dear Flory: That is the first time anybody wants my signature for something else than sign a check. So it is a pleasure to give you this little sample, though I resent the remark that I write small letters. Besides I am looking forward to your visit. We are snowed in again, wished I would be now in Puerto Rico.

11/29/64 Love yours Ernst H. Rosenbaum.

Noted dermatologist Dr. Ernst Rosenbaum expresses consistency and practicality in the evenly spaced margins of this writing sample. The fact that he never omits an "i" dot—all are placed directly above the stem—indicates that he is also systematic and conscientious, all valuable traits for a man of the medical profession.

Chapter 4

PEN PRESSURE

The Degree of Energy, Aggressiveness, Emotion, Health

The variations of pen pressure reveal mental and physical vitality, as well as depth of feeling. Pen pressure also tells whether a person is timid and retiring, or aggressive and outgoing.

Heavy pen-pressure writers take a long time to forget an experience deeply felt. Light-pressure writers, on the other hand, may get just as excited as heavier ones at the moment; but they are able to forget about it all much faster.

Samples written with a fountain pen are the best for an analysis, since pressure does not show as well with a ball-point. Pencil samples should never be evaluated. People usually select the pen point that reflects their personality—thin and delicate for the quiet, retiring person; or broad and heavy for the energetic and intense.

If the pen is faulty, such as those frequently found in post offices, it can produce blotches and sputters that are misleading. Fortunately, people seldom write at length with a faulty pen.

PEN PRESSURE

1. Thin	Thin pen pressure	Shallow, timid, modest, fatigued
2. Extremely thin	Extremely thin	Irresolute, ailing, reluctant, reserved

3. Medium	medium pressure	Conforming, composed, adaptable, unaffected
4. Heavy	heavy pressure	Energetic, aggressive, sensitive, impulsive
5. Extremely heavy	extremely heavy	Emphatic, forceful, domineering, sensual
6. Irregular	thin and heavy	Unstable, insincere, unreliable, ailing
7. Heavy, muddy, smeary	heavy muddy smeary	Deceitful, violent, drug/crime-prone

■

Arturo Morales Carrion, Consultant to the Secretary of the Organization of American States.

The small, angular writing of this young Puerto Rican-born diplomat and administrator reflects a keen and critical insight. And the heavy pen pressure and firm underscoring reveal that he is a self-assured, determined man, with a good deal of initiative.

PABLO CASALS, world-famed Catalonian cellist and composer.

Johann Sebastian Bach.

His music lives in the highest summits of human creation

Pablo Casals

The firm, clear script of this remarkable artist indicates his definite, direct nature. These traits are also revealed by the fact that, at the age of eighty-eight, he is still the "maestro" of the cello, an instrument that demands of its player extraordinary strength and precision. The heavy pen pressure expresses profound feeling, and the many printed letters, in an otherwise longhand writing, show his excellent sense of aesthetics—qualities of great importance to any artist.

I well recall the amazing accuracy of your analysis of my handwriting one evening in the Caribe Hilton Hotel.

I am sure your book will be a remarkable success.

Sincerely –
John A. Notte Jr.

John A. Notte, Jr., former governor of Rhode Island.

The script of this successful politician, now returned to private law practice, reveals many of the traits that have led to his success in both fields. The heavy pen pressure and the angular, pointed letters "m" and "n" show determination, and an alert, active mind. The firm downstrokes are signs of his intensity and decisiveness.

Chapter 5

SIZE OF WRITING

The Degree of Sociability, Modesty, Patience

After passing the grade-school days of writing big, round practice letters on a sheet of tablet paper, each person tends to write with a surprisingly consistent letter size. There may be temporary variations from this general letter-size habit caused by momentary alterations of a person's mood. But taken as a whole, his script will probably fall into either the small, medium, or large category.

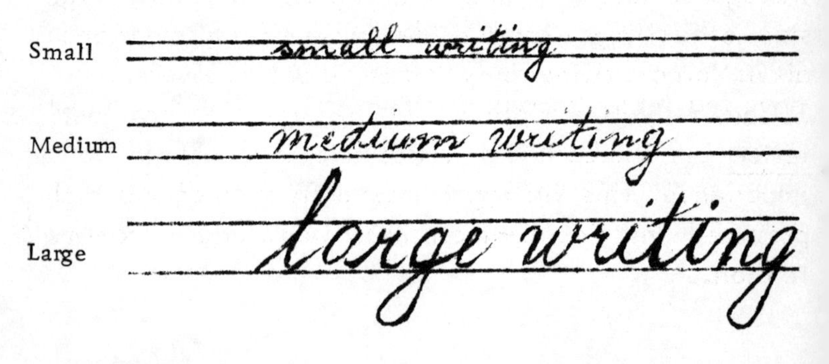

The other letter-size groups, closely related to the three categories mentioned, are "very small," "very large," and a third in which the size constantly fluctuates from one type to another.

Small writing is the sign of a person with an analytical mind. Writers of this sort, usually modest and restrained people, have the patience to concentrate on tasks that involve detailed work.

Writers whose letters are very small are also reserved and modest, and are usually even more patiently methodical than those whose writing is merely small.

People whose writing falls consistently in the medium-size range are often adaptable and conforming.

Large-sized writing is found in the writing of people who are enterprising, spontaneous, and venturesome. They do not care to attend to details and are restless, sometimes erratic and temperamental. If large writing is rounded and graceful, it is expressive of sociability. If it is angular and sharp, there is energy indicated, but the sociability is lessened, and the writer is probably more critical and hard-driving.

Extra-large writing is seen among people who have a persuasive way of talking and who like to be admired, such as many people in the entertainment world. They often have a materialistic nature and are usually extravagant, tolerant, and pretentious. This extra-large size of writing expresses the same trends mentioned about large writing, only in a more extreme sense.

Considerable variations in the size of individual letters are indicative of restlessness, inconsistency, and impatience. This writing is frequently seen among high pressured individuals—those who work under extreme tension.

SIZE

1. Small	small writing	Analytical, restrained, intelligent, modest
2. Very small	very small writing	Unassuming, reserved, scholastic, methodical
3. Medium	medium writing	Adaptable, conforming, unassuming

4. Large	large	Enterprising, sociable, spontaneous, restless
5. Extremely large	Extremely	Sociable, materialistic, extravagant, pretentious
6. Variation: small, medium, large	small, large	Speedy, inconsistent, enterprising, impatient

The small letters "e" and "r", written larger in proportion to the other small letters in the writing, indicate vanity, preoccupation with self-importance, and possibly a fondness for material, money-making matters.

Remember the warnings made earlier in the book: Don't jump to conclusions about the writer of the sample you are examining. If, for example, a person's writing size fluctuates a lot within the sample, you can suspect that he is inconsistent. But you should not definitely stamp him as such, until you see whether other features—such as his writing slant and base line—also prove him to have that characteristic.

XAVIER CUGAT

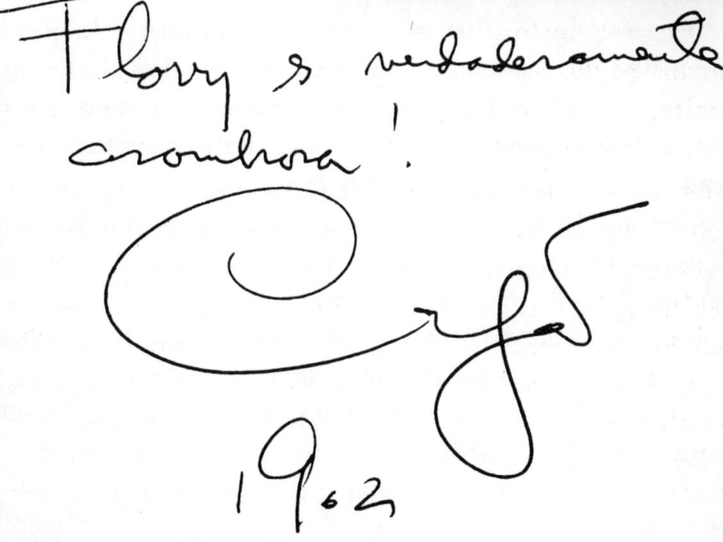

The large-size, angular writing of the well-known Xavier Cugat, whose name is a tradition in music, expresses a hard-driving, enterprising nature. The inflated, rhythmic loops in this script portray a vivid imagination, a truly distinctive sense of musical interpretation, and a highly articulate individuality in both thought and action.

Chapter 6

ANGULAR AND ROUNDED TOPS AND BASES

The Degree of Patience, Perception, Aggressiveness

Angular tops and bases are seen in the handwriting of perceptive, energetic, and persistent people. A person who forms angular letters is not easily swayed. He often is considered firm and aggressive.

Rounded letter tops, on the other hand, often express an easy-going, indecisive nature. Letters rounded at the base indicate patience and kindness.

A handwriting with angular and rounded letter formations shows a combination of traits. It may express perception, as well as kindness and tact.

The frequency of either angular or rounded formations will determine the predominant traits of the writer.

You may find an occasional instance of what is called "square writing." This type of letter formation—square, box-like tops and bases—marks a writer as having mechanical or inventive ability.

ANGULAR AND ROUNDED

1. Angular tops — Energetic, aggressive, perceptive, persistent
2. Angular bases — Firm, persistent, critical, impatient

Formation	Traits
3. Angular tops and bases	Perceptive, impatient, aggressive, critical
4. Rounded tops (Arcades)	Easy-going, patient, drifting, irresolute
5. Rounded bases (Garlands)	Adaptable, kind, patient, sociable
6. Rounded tops and bases	Easy-going, kind, sociable, irresolute
7. Combined tops and bases	Perceptive, kind, critical, patient
8. Square tops and/or bases	Inventive, mechanically dexterous

■

Sincere best wishes for success in your literary accomplishment.

Yolanda Garcia

This script of a private secretary to a hotel manager reveals good reasoning, eloquence, and an imaginative bent, as expressed in the combination of connected and disconnected letters within the words. The angular letter formation "m", "n", and "t" show rapidity of thought and action, as well as initiative—certainly excellent qualities for a top-notch secretary.

at the uncanniness of your reading. We wish you the fullest success with your forthcoming book.

Hoping to see you in the near future, I remain,

Respectfully,

Paul P. Rao

Tax Commissioner Paul P. Rao, Jr., at thirty, is the youngest full commissioner in the history of New York City's government. The angular writing and underscoring of his signature reveal keen perception, self-assurance, and initiative. The forward slant expresses a spontaneous, friendly personality.

■

There may be such a thing as destiny. But we must act as if all were the product of man's effort.

Joel Magruder

The many connected letters in the handwriting of Joel Magruder, law student and reporter for the San Juan Star, show that he has good reasoning power, and the ability to think things through from start to finish. The angular formation of the letters "m" and "n" are signs of a keen, perceptive mind, and the printed unadorned capital letters indicate a creative nature that shuns pretense or formality.

HANK KETCHAM

Dear Miss Nadall—

Sorry I have taken so long answering your letter. Here's hoping that the enclosed is sufficient and that your forthcoming book enjoys huge success.

Sincerely yours—

Hank Ketcham

Hank Ketcham, creator of the universally popular "Dennis the Menace," is a man of keen perception. This trait shows vividly in the many angular letters "m", "n", "u", and "w" in his script.

Ketcham is also a man of marked originality. His capital letters, formed in a printlike manner, and the high "t" crosses are signs of both originality and creative ability—traits just as important as perception to a cartoonist who distils rich humor from the everyday antics of children.

Chapter 7

SPACING BETWEEN LINES AND WORDS

The Degree of Self-Assurance, Sociability, Tolerance, Economy

Spacing between lines and words refers to the space that is left between the individual words in a line, and the space between each separate line of writing.

Even spacing between lines and words is a sign of consistency, good judgment, and emotional stability.

Uneven spacing between lines and words is indicative of emotional instability, carelessness as to details, or a poor sense of economy.

No spacing (or nearly none) between lines and words reflects a person with set ideas, who is intolerant, reserved, cautious, and economical, possibly thrifty.

Wide spacing between lines and words is seen among people who are self-confident, determined, impatient, liberal, and sociable.

Extremely wide spacing between lines and words is expressive of self-assurance, enterprise, tolerance, sociability, and possibly some shallowness and extravagance. People who space in this fashion usually have many acquaintances, yet they seldom have close ties to anyone and often feel lonely.

A writer who spaces the words evenly and spaces the lines unevenly (or the reverse) shows that he has both favorable and unfavorable traits. He can be self-assured, sociable, tolerant, but also restless and inconsistent. Illustrations follow:

SPACING

Type	Sample	Traits
1. Even	Even spacing	Consistent, stable, reliable, rational
2. Uneven	uneven spacing	Inconsistent, careless, unstable, disorganized
3. No (or nearly none)	no spacing	Economical, reserved, intolerant, cautious
4. Wide	wide spacing	Liberal, responsive, confident, sociable
5. Extremely wide	extremely wide	Enterprising, shallow, extravagant, tolerant

■

This script of my father, Hugo Fridberg, written one month before his death at age eighty-three, displays will power and drive extraordinary in a man of his years. The extended writing reveals spontaneity and confidence, while the evenly spaced lines and words show good reasoning. The angular letter formation expresses his alert mentality. Some letters (1, 2, 3) show a creative bent, which was manifested in the numerous articles he wrote for the German-language newspapers *Aufbau*, *Staats Zeitung*, and *Herold*.

VICTOR BORGE

Someone once said that Victor Borge is the world's "funniest man." The abilities and traits that have worked to push him to the highest ranks of artists and comedians show clearly in his writing. The excellent proportion in the spacing between lines and words bespeaks a man who has a knack for timing and balance. The heavy pen pressure and firm downstrokes (as in the letters "y", "p", and "g") denote intensity and decisiveness, while the precisely placed "i" dots express dependability and care with details.

There are many hazards in an excessive use of punishment. The parent or teacher who relies often upon punishment may be emotionally upset and may be expressing aggression by victimizing a helpless child.

Chapter 8

EXTENDED AND COMPRESSED WORDS

The Degree of Sociability, Aggressiveness, Economy

Extension and compression refer to the degree of separation between the letters within a word. It should not be mistaken for "Spacing Between Lines and Words" (Chapter 7).

The extension or compression within a word expresses social attitude—be it introversion, extroversion, or somewhere between these extremes. It is also an indicator of a sense of economy, and reveals the spontaneity of response to new ideas and ventures.

WORDS

1. Compressed	compressed	Critical, cautious, economical, inhibited
2. Extended	extended	Enterprising, liberal, sociable, confident
3. Compressed and extended	compress-extend	Sociable, economical, confident, critical

Resist the impulse to classify a person as "inhibited" or "enterprising" just because one word is either compressed or extended. Look closely at all the words in the sample of writing you have before you. Are they predominantly compressed, or are most of them extended, within the definitions of these writing habits in the illustrations?

Also remember to compare what this feature of writing tells you with what you have learned about the writer from other features of his writing, as described in the other chapters of this book. Any definitive character trait will show up in many different ways in a person's script.

■

your book and your
analysis. This is a risk
I am taking but do it
gladly in the interest
of your scientific research.
Best wishes

Sincerely

Michael V. Di Salle

Columbus, Ohio

Michael V. Di Salle, former Governor of Ohio and well-known humanitarian, expresses in his extended writing a liberal, responsive, and initiatory nature. The fact that some letters within the words are connected, while others are disconnected, is a sign of fluency of thought and expression, of good reasoning powers tempered with a dose of intuition.

Chapter 9

CONNECTED AND DISCONNECTED LETTERS WITHIN WORDS

The Degree of Concentration, Versatility, Originality

Connected letters—seven or more—written together without lifting the pen, express fluency of thought and speech, and appear in the script of people who are able to think from origin to consequence, concentrate well, and are gifted with good reasoning power.

Disconnected letters—not consecutively joined together—reveal either a lack of concentration, shallowness or an inventive, original mind with a creative bent. These writers act frequently on impulse.

Writing that varies and is composed of connected and disconnected letters within the word implies that the writer is versatile. He may be endowed with good reasoning power, and may be creative, although he may lack the ability to concentrate.

The predominance of either connected or disconnected letters identifies his predominant characteristic.

LETTERS		
1. Connected	Connected	Rational, eloquent, analytical, logical
2. Disconnected	many disconnected	Shallow, creative, intuitive, impulsive
3. Connected and disconnected	connected and disconnected	Eloquent, versatile, creative, rational

analyst, citizen of the world, and
adopted Puerto Rican.
Jose H. Amadeo M.D.
12 March 1963.

Dr. Jose H. Amadeo, Chief Surgeon, Veterans' Hospital, Puerto Rico.

The well-proportioned script of this eminent surgeon, and the many connected letters, written without lifting the pen (1, 2, 3), are signs of the thorough reasoning that enables him to think from cause to consequence. The angular letters "m" and "n" express a keen perception. The forward slant is a mark of a friendly, sympathetic nature.

▪

que la tierra era plana y no se
habia llegado a conoser la mitad
del mundo.
gran parte de asia y la parte n
formaban las unicas tierras co
apas existentes entonses eran in

Convicted of first-degree murder.

This spiritless, shaky writing reveals inconsistency and a lack of ambition. The downslanting "t" crosses (3, 6, 7) show a domineering nature. The many connected letters within words (7, 8, 9) express a mind capable of thinking out problems from start to finish. Judging from this writing sample, the crime was probably planned.

FRANCIS CARDINAL SPELLMAN

The forward-slanting writing, and the gently rounded letters "a" and "o" of Cardinal Spellman's autograph (on apron) are clear keynotes to his kind and friendly personality. The straight formation of the letter "F" with the firm cross-strokes shows self-assurance, independence, and initiative. The Cardinal is a man who reasons things through from cause to consequence, as indicated by the many connected letters within the words.

(This handwriting specimen, consisting of only a few words, is adequate for merely a brief personality sketch.)

Chapter 10

SIGNATURE

The Symbol of the Outer Personality

Signatures are a very important and most frequently written combination of letters. They reveal the outer personality, the face that people show to others.

A person's signature does not always remain the same through the course of his adult life. As his life changes his personality through the years, so also may his personality effect changes in the signature (as well as in the general writing). Banks are particularly aware of these changes. Occasionally they call their clients in to verify signatures that have varied greatly from the original samples on file.

Signatures that are plain, distinct, and unadorned (as well as those with clear-cut underscoring) indicate a sincere, stable, and unpretentious person.

Signatures that are lavishly flourished and ornamental are found in the writing of showy, conceited, and secretive people.

Indistinct, illegible signatures are signs of carelessness, evasiveness, and discretion; these writers do not care to disclose any of their concerns or problems.

Some people connect the first and last name of their signatures, and write them all in one word; these people also prefer discretion and object to being questioned.

Signatures that diminish into a threadlike line belong to people who are impatient with delays, who often find ingenious ways to avert obstacles, and may be shrewd in their dealings.

Final strokes that stretch into straight lines, fill in blank spaces, or loop around the ending of signatures—for that matter, any unnecessary end strokes—have a special significance. Straight-line endings show a cautious or perhaps economical bent. Endings that loop or circle about are signs of an eccentric, discreet, suspicious, or possibly grasping nature.

SIGNATURE

1. Plain, distinct, legible	Sincere, reliable, modest, unpretentious
2. Indistinct, illegible, intertwined	Evasive, cunning, misrepresenting
3. Encircled, half-circled, surrounded	Secretive, grasping, selfish, tenacious
4. Lavishly flourished, ornamental, knotted	Pretentious, conceited, secretive, eccentric
5. First and last name connected	Secretive, active, independent, critical
6. Ending strokes diminishing	Enterprising, hasty, shrewd, diplomatic
7. Ending strokes fill in blank spaces	Self-assured, critical, secretive, suspicious

I was born in Turkey in
July 30, 1927 -

The script of this Turkish-born structural engineer, Constanti Dinos, clearly reveals the abilities and traits that have made him successful in his field. The original, printed letters "D", "T", and "k" indicate imagination and creativeness. The "y" ending in "Turkey" and "July" is formed like a number 7. This writing habit indicates calculative abilities.

■

to talk English and Spanish and
my teacher tells me that I
can Speak and Spell English well

1963

The writing of Olympia Perez Daple, eight-year-old girl, shows great intelligence and a degree of maturity surprising in a child her age. Alertness and keen perception are expressed by the angular letters "m" and "n". The original way in which she connects the capital letters of her names shows a good deal of independence, self-assurance, and tenacity.

Chapter 11

UNDERSCORING AND ENCIRCLING OF SIGNATURES

Emphasis in the Symbol of the Outer Personality

Underscoring or encircling of a signature is an emphatic gesture and an additional stroke(s) to the actual signature. Any unnecessary strokes have a particular significance.

In evaluating underscoring and encircling more accurately, compare them with other writing habits in the signature that may stress, deny, or modify the interpretation.

UNDERSCORING

1. Straight line(s) above or under	Mr. Liner	Independent, ambitious, self-confident, resolute
2. Straight line(s) divided by dashes, dots	Mr. Dasher Mr. Dot	Industrious, emphatic, self-assured, reliable
3. Wavy line with or without dashes or dots	Mr. Wavy	Humorous, imaginative, original, romantic

	Signature	Traits
4.	Circle surrounding signature	Secretive, grasping, tenacious, selfish
5.	Lavishly flourished, ornamental circles	Eccentric, conceited, secretive, pretentious
6.	Illegible, crossed-out signature	Concealed, evasive, mistrusting, deceitful
7.	Hooked line above or under	Persistent, domineering, realistic, initiatory
8.	Zigzag underscoring	Original, resolute, alert, industrious
9.	Spiral, corkscrew underscoring	Eccentric, evasive, self-assured, active
10.	Twined	Cunning, eccentric, evasive, distrustful
11.	Encircled	Pretentious, secretive, self-centered, vain

SENATOR LUIS MUNOZ MARIN,
former Governor
of Puerto Rico.

Los pueblos deben tener confianza en sí mismos, y es nuestra misión que el puertorriqueño la tenga.

Luis Muñoz Marín
1963

The angular writing and the heavy pen pressure of the first elected Governor of Puerto Rico express an energetic and emphatic nature. The long, hooked cross stroke above his signature reveals perseverance, and a great deal of initiative, as the history of his rise to power in the world of politics well confirms.

El sentido de justicia en el juez se mide por el sentido de lo justo en el hombre comun

Hon. Luis Negron Fernandez, Chief Justice, Supreme Court, Puerto Rico.

Thorough reasoning, seen in the many connected letters in this script, is only one of the traits with which this eminent jurist is endowed. The Greek letter "e" (in "el") indicates cultural and literary interest, common to many scholars. Keen perception shows in the angular formation of the letters "m" and "n". And the underscoring points out confidence and persistent will power.

■

Ramon Cancel Negron, Puerto Rican State Department official.

The angular writing and heavy pen pressure of this affable Puerto Rican functionary show quick perception, determination, and initiative. The straight line in the signature indicates self-confidence and an ambitious nature.

■

By now you may enjoy a feeling akin to that first glow of satisfaction a portrait painter feels when he sees the rough-brushed outline of his painting well placed on the canvas. Having grasped the meaning of the basic features of handwriting analysis, you are now able to discover fundamental character traits of people whose handwriting you examine.

These traits are the outline for a picture of a person's nature. They are vitally important to your analysis of that person, just as a painter's rough sketch on the canvas is vital to his purpose. If the base of either an analysis or a painting is faulty, the structure built upon that base will be unsound.

Neither the artist nor a person sincerely concerned with learning the meanings of handwriting, however, will stop with merely an outline. The details yet to be revealed are also of cardinal importance. The artist works in small strokes to capture the precise shadow of an eyebrow or a flesh tone. You also will want to "capture" the meaning of the small details of handwriting—for example, the way the "i"s are dotted and "t"s are crossed.

These small but very important gestures of handwriting are set down and illustrated for you in Part II, "Individual Features." You may be in for many surprising revelations about yourself, your friends and associates as you proceed through the coming pages.

PART II

INDIVIDUAL FEATURES

Individual features of handwriting are like
the fine details of a finished portrait:
they are small strokes that fill in the outline
and bring out the person's unique individuality.

HOW TO ESTABLISH DETAIL CHARACTERISTICS

Normal Reactions, Mixed Emotions, Potentialities

The growth of human character is one of the most fascinatingly complex processes encountered on this earth. Psychiatrists have been able in recent decades to unravel the once inscrutable fabric of character growth and discover the influences that at different times have worked to make each man what he is today.

The discovery of a way back through mental time has forced us today to realize that each human is no monolithic character type. No reasonable person, will, in our time, say simply that another human is "good" or "bad," except when speaking in the most offhand fashion. Any serious attempt to describe a fellow human should take into account the background against which he was reared, the social forces with which he has had to contend, and the hereditary equipment given him at birth.

In his handwriting, a person will show himself far more complicated a being than his outward appearance may suggest. And the individual features of his script, which are described in this part of the book, are the places where all the secret corners of his character are made manifest.

The individual features will show far more diversity

than the basic features, which were explained in Part I. This is but natural, since the basic features trace the fundamental outlines of character—which generally remain far more constant than do the smaller details of a person's inner self.

You may find for example that a writer will cross his "t"s in several fashions in one sample of writing. As is pointed out in the first chapter of this part, such variety is a sign not so much of instability as it is of a versatile mind. Of course, you will want to know more about a person than the mere fact that he is versatile. To do this, the best method is a continuation of the method suggested in Part I.

First, see what types of letter formation are present in the sample you are examining. Then isolate the types that appear with greatest frequency in the script. Jot down the alternative meanings that follow the illustrations of the particular writing habit.

As you make notes for each successive aspect of the individual features, some traits among the alternatives will appear more constantly than others. These, then, will be the ones you can say with certainty the writer possesses. In this way you will avoid the perils of snap judgment.

"T" CROSSES

The "t" cross is one of the most important master keys to analysis of a writing specimen. There are surprisingly many ways in which this simple, yet meaning-packed stroke may vary from one writer to the next.

In fact, a person may, in one writing sample, cross the "t"s in several different manners. This reveals versatility, often originality, and a responsive, active nature. The more frequently-appearing "t" crosses determine the predominant character trait.

A writer who crosses his "t"s in the same way throughout the entire writing script is consistent, systematic, and often conforming.

"T" CROSSES

1. Evenly crossed — Consistent, systematic

2. Thin — Indecisive, conforming

3. Heavy	Self-assured, determined
4. Extremely heavy, firm, long	Domineering, aggressive
5. Left side of stem	Reluctant, procrastinating
6. Right side of stem	Impulsive, impatient, speedy
7. Low	Quick-acting, sympathetic
8. High	Premeditative, imaginative
9. Slanting upward	Optimistic, ambitious
10. Slanting downward	Obstinate, domineering
11. Encircled	Jealous, selfish, grasping
12. Knotted, looped	Secretive, literary, persistent

13. Sharp, angular — Persistent, active, sensitive

14. Hooked — Realistic, initiatory, persistent

15. Wavy — Humorous, tolerant

16. Printed, x-like  Creative, independent, inventive

17. Club-like starting — High-strung, explosive, impulsive

18. Club-like ending — Obstinate, violent, tyrannical, brutal

19. Umbrella-curved — Self-reliant, original, ambitious

20. Bowl-curved — Drifting, weak-willed, shallow

21. Omitted — Careless, absent-minded, impatient

What has been said about the "t" crosses applies also to the cross strokes of the capital letter "F".

ABBE LANE

The unique, graceful upper loops in the capital letters of this universally popular entertainer reveal the excellent sense of showmanship—an ability which keeps her at the top in her field. The originally-formed letters "T" and "F" express her individuality and creativeness. And the firm downstrokes show a well-developed critical sense, self-assurance, and determination.

Chapter 2

CAPITAL LETTER "M"

The capital letter "M" is an important and the most revealing single letter in handwriting analysis. It is formed in a great many different ways, contributing much information concerning character traits and aptitudes.

The capital letter "M" is composed of three down strokes. These strokes vary frequently in their relative height to one another. Each individual height, in comparison with the others, reveals a specific trait.

If the first stroke is somewhat higher than the other two, it expresses independence and pride.

But, if the first stroke is a great deal higher than the others, it indicates excessive pride, vanity, and intellectual conceit.

A capital letter "M" with all strokes equally high, shows a well-balanced, adaptable, and unassuming nature.

If the second stroke, or third, or both, are higher than the first stroke, desires, memories, or fears in a hidden form exert a ruling influence upon a person. This holds particularly true if the third stroke is a great deal higher than the others.

A printed capital letter "M" (like any printed letter in a longhand writing), is a sign of individual, creative ideas and an independent mind.

If the capital letter "M" is formed in a variety of ways in a specimen of writing, it shows versatility. This writer will have many interests.

What has been said about the letter "M" applies also to the letter "N".

Some of the more familiar styles of the letter "M" are illustrated here. Other styles can be evaluated by comparing them with the chapters on features that describe the particular peculiarity of their formation. For example, the letter "M" written with angular formations should be compared with the chapter on Angular Writing; or a small, knotted loop in this letter should be evaluated with the help of the chapter on Small, Knotted Loops.

"M" STROKE

1. First higher than others		Independent, confident, self-esteeming
2. Extremely high		Opinionated, vain, conceited, critical
3. Second, third higher than first		Indecisive, skeptical, complex, frustrated
4. Evenly high		Unassuming, well-balanced, tactful
5. Wavy <u>initial</u>		Responsive, humorous, tolerant

6. Backstroke initial — Sensitive, proud, secretive, critical

7. Curled initial — Jealous, self-centered, cautious

8. Curled final — Timid, tenacious, jealous, selfish

9. Curled final past base line — Cowardly, jealous, prejudiced, selfish

10. Rounded at base line — Kind, adaptable, cautious, patient

11. Downward abrupt final — Impatient, self-assured, critical

12.	Down to right final past base line	Sarcastic, short-tempered, obstinate
13.	Ornamental, flourished	Pretentious, eccentric, conceited, imaginative
14.	Printed, original	Creative, inventive, independent, original

Chapter 3

SMALL LETTERS "a", "o", "d", "g"

The various formations of the small letters "a", "o", "d", and "g" are often more revealing than many other aspects of a handwriting. They can express some very favorable, as well as some decidedly unfavorable, character traits.

Although the letters "d" and "g" of this group have upper and lower loops, we are here concerned only with the portion written immediately above the base line. This area is commonly called the "middle zone" as is shown in the diagram below. These letters, in their middle zone, reveal among other traits the writer's tendency toward candor or deceit, toward sincerity or secretiveness.

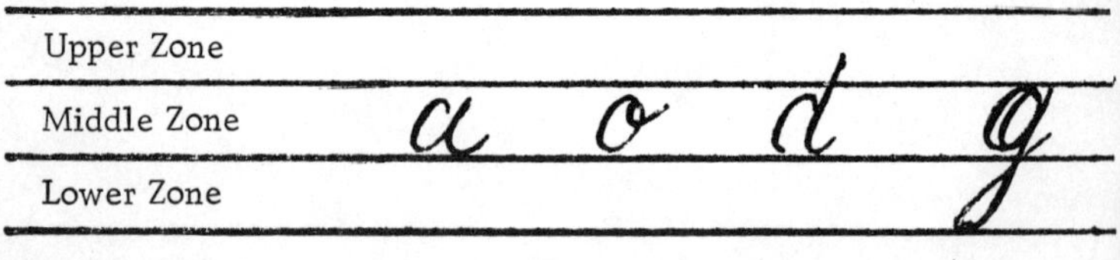

Upper Zone
Middle Zone a o d g
Lower Zone

The degree to which these letters are open or closed at the top of the middle zone is a gauge of the degree to which a person is "open" or "closed" in his attitude toward other people.

If they are rounded in formation, they tell of a warm-hearted disposition; if squeezed, they are signs of a less friendly, more critical temperament.

These letters, if frequently open at the bottom (fortunately a rare occurrence in handwriting), point out some extremely undesirable traits, such as deceit and a tendency to antisocial behavior.

Double-curved ovals, or little knotlike loops inserted in the middle-zone portion of these letters, bring to light idiosyncrasies of character that may sometimes be concealed from others.

The most frequently encountered formations of these letters are illustrated in this chapter.

a, o, d, g (Middle Zone)

1. Closed on top and bottom	Secretive, diplomatic
2. Open at top	Trusting, frank
3. Rounded	Friendly, warm-hearted
4. Squeezed	Critical, impatient
5. Knotted, small-looped (closed)	Suspicious, secretive
6. Double-knotted loop (closed)	Evasive, distorted

7.	Double-curved	Skeptical, elusive
8.	Retraced, added strokes, loops	Evasive, insincere
9.	Oval sliced by initial stroke (closed)	Cunning, untrustworthy
10.	Open at <u>bottom</u>	Deceitful, crime-prone
11.	Stenciled, beadlike	Deceitful, ailing, drug-prone
12.	Oval clogged with ink	Drug prone, sexually unrestricted

Never pass judgment on a single appearance of a letter formation, particularly when it expresses an unfavorable trait. If the unfavorable sign is merely occasional, the writer may have only a tendency to slip now and then into the bad trait mentioned, but otherwise observe favorable attitudes and conduct.

Sixty-five-year-old cancer patient, Veterans' Hospital, Puerto Rico.

The writing of this man, afflicted with cancer of the bladder, shows signs in the tiny beadlike swellings of letters "m", and "o" in ("fumo") and in the zero in ("50"), of severe changes in normal bodily functions. The generally shaky aspect of the writing, and the letters that seem to fall over forward, indicate that, in addition to his physical affliction, he has symptoms of mental disorder.

■

Convicted of grand larceny.

The shaky strokes, the uneven pen pressure, and the muddy writing indicate a warped, distorted mind. The tendency to be dishonest is apparent from the sliced ovals and retraced letters (1, 2, 4, 6). The many connected letters within words (7, 8, 9) show that this writer thinks with a semblance of logic, but he may reach weird conclusions.

THE HON. FELISA RINCON GAUTIER,
Mayor of San Juan, Puerto Rico.

To Flory
Very happy to show you my
handwriting.
Sincerely,
Felisa R. Gautier

The script of San Juan's mayor, and "Woman of the Americas," shows a rare combination of strength, will power, kindness, and sympathy. The "t" crosses placed high up on the stems in her writing indicate long-range planning and enthusiasm. The manner in which she rounds her letters "o" and "a", as well as the forward slant, show warmth and friendliness.

Chapter 4

"I" DOTS

The little touch of the dot over the "i" can bring to light unsuspected characteristics of the writer.

The "i" dot can reveal the degree of concentration, exactness, procrastination, originality, eccentricity, imagination, patience, and temper.

Variations of "i" dots in one writing specimen show versatility. The more often-repeated "i" dots determine which is the predominant characteristic.

What is explained about the "i" dot applies also to the "j" dot. The more frequent formations are illustrated here.

"I" DOTS

1. Directly above stem		Systematic, concientious
2. Very high	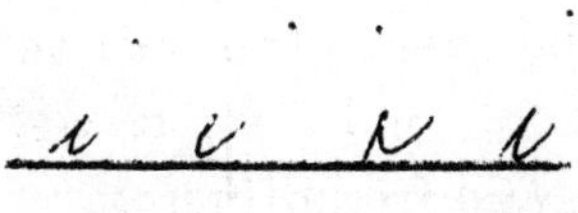	Imaginative, unrealistic

3. Left of stem — Drifting, procrastinating

4. Right of stem — Progressive, impatient

5. Light — Nonaggressive, cautious

6. Heavy — Aggressive, materialistic

7. Circled — Imaginative, original

8. Dashed — Vivacious, irritable

9. Downward-dashed — Obstinate, tempered

10. Wavy — Humorous, witty

11. Omitted — Careless, absent-minded

WELBY VAN HORN,
Caribe Hilton tennis pro.

FREDERICO DE JESUS SCHUCK

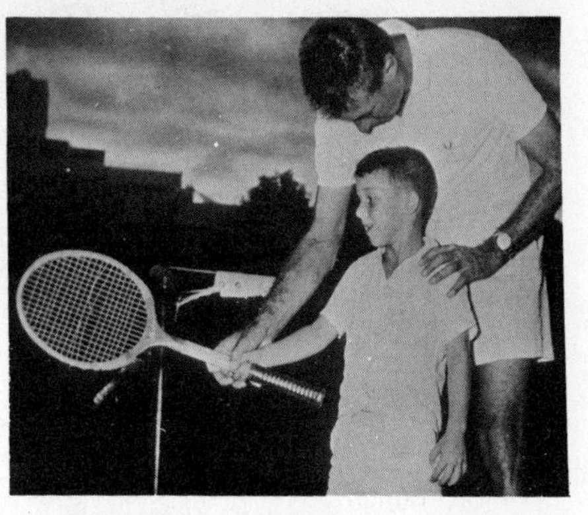

I would like to be a champion.

Federico de Jesús Schuck.

Eight-year-old Frederico de Jesus is one of Welby's most promising young tennis devotees. The heavy pen pressure and the well-placed, firm "t" crosses tell of his determination, endurance, and physical strength.

Holder of a number of United States professional tennis championship titles, Welby's writing is a detailed list of his talents for outstanding sportsmanship. The long lower loops indicate a love of outdoor activity. A keen perception is expressed in the angular writing. His meticulous attention to detail and his constancy — two very valuable traits for a trainer of young skills — are evident in his habit of never omitting the "i" dots.

A Caribe Hilton friend of long standing. Wishing you every success with your book.

Sincerely

Welby Van Horn

Chapter 5

INITIAL AND FINAL STROKES

The seemingly insignificant gestures of initial and final strokes of words can reveal amazingly distinct attitudes of a writer.

Long initial strokes frequently relate to the past. Many people in whose writing they appear live bound by the tradition of their early years. Long initial strokes can also indicate people who are sentimental, touchy, suspicious, or immature and resentful.

If initial strokes are long and rounded, as well as thin in pen pressure, they express skepticism or immaturity—as is often seen in the handwriting of young people.

Initial strokes that are long, but straight and inflexible show resentment of conditions or environment, and possibly an opinionated, or quarrelsome nature.

Curled-in initial strokes point out nonaggression, caution, and egotism, as well as jealousy.

Omitted initial strokes are signs of simplicity, independence, fluency of thought, and a well-developed, progressive mind.

When initial strokes appear in some words and are omitted in others, diversified characteristics are expressed. The writer may be independent in certain ways and not in others; he may have a good, progressive mind, but also be opinionated and resentful at times.

Final strokes of words are formed in an unlimited variety of ways. There are many more different final strokes than initial strokes seen in handwriting. Each of the individual final strokes expresses a specific character trait.

Some of the more frequently appearing initial and final strokes are illustrated here.

INITIAL STROKE

1. Rounded	Immature, skeptical
2. Straight, from below base line	Resentful, suspicious, touchy
3. Hooked	Persistant, grasping
4. Wavy	Humorous, tolerant
5. Backstroke	Sensitive, vain, critical
6. Curled in	Self-centered, jealous, cautious
7. Omitted	Independent, keen, initiatory, active

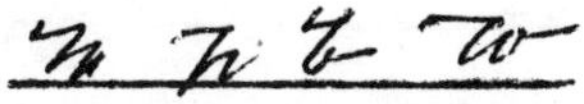

FINAL STROKES

Stroke	Meaning
1. Raised up	Optimistic, daring
2. Raised high up	Imaginative, fanatical
3. Curled over backward	Tenacious, egotistic
4. Small, knotted loop	Literary, imaginative
5. Curled backward	Clannish, egotistic
6. Straight backward	Selfish, intolerant
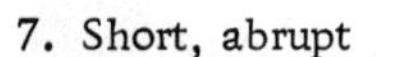 7. Short, abrupt	Impatient, decisive
8. Down past base line	Decisive, impulsive
9. Down to right	Obstinate, short-tempered
10. Club-like	Violent, brutal
11. Down, forward to right	Initiatory, impatient, speedy

12. Filling blank space	e m d	Critical, suspicious
13. Spiraled	g t m	Eccentric, evasive
14. Rounded	e a n d	Kind, humane, considerate
15. Curled back	e a n d	Self-centered, intolerant
16. Curled in	e n a d	Tenacious, timid, jealous
17. Hooked	g a n d	Opinionated, spiteful

■

How amazing you are
to be able to see inside
of me without X-ray
eyes, but with the
unique ability to read
my handwriting!
Judy [illegible]

This balanced script of a social worker, with the many connected letters within words, shows good reasoning. The angular writing expresses keen perception and initiative, while the long, rounded final strokes indicate an interest in humanity.

Chapter 6

UPPER AND LOWER LOOPS

Loops in handwriting are as fascinating as the most outspoken exposé magazine. Some point out the writer who is realistic, or who is lost in the realms of spiritual fantasy; with others, you can spot in a flash the person who is athletically inclined or has physical debility, as well as one who is absorbed in a world of material or sensual desires.

Since there are several kinds of loops to be examined, you should first know that the upper and lower loops are made in two of the three distinct handwriting zones illustrated below.

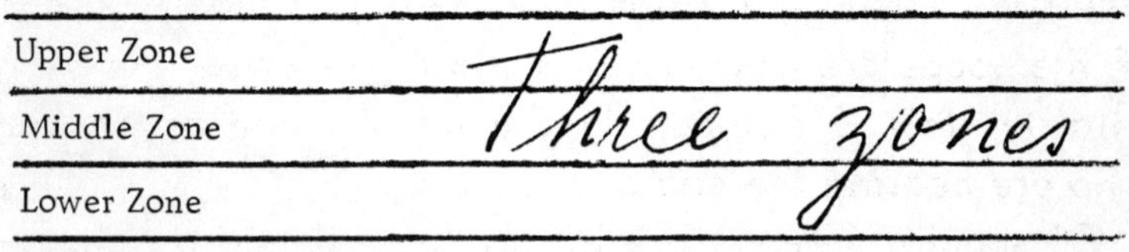

Upper Zone
Middle Zone
Lower Zone

Three zones

The portion of letters that penetrates into the upper zone is called "upper loop." Letters that commonly penetrate into the lower zone have what are called "lower loops."

The middle zone is left for the small letters and the mid-portion of upper- and lower-looped letters.

There are three general varieties of upper loops. The <u>low</u> upper loops indicate the humble disposition of a more submissive or unimaginative person. Moderately high loops show realism and self-assurance. The very high, often inflated loops, are signs of a mind given to excessive pride, imagination, keen vision, or fantasy and perhaps fanaticism.

Looped stems in the upper zone of the letters "d" and "t" express a sensitive, critical nature.

Omitted upper loops are signs of a progressive and active mind.

The lower loops belong to the physical drives and material interests.

Full lower loops are signs of physical strength and a stress on material, money-making matters. If they are full and inflated, and also written with heavy pen pressure, they indicate a strong sexual drive.

Long, moderately wide or narrow lower loops appear in the writing of restless, active people, and athletes.

Loops that run into the written line above, or tangle into the letters of the line below are the result of a confused mind, or of emotional instability.

Weak and wavy lower loops are marks of physical debility, often seen in the handwriting of older people. If the loops are quavery and short, the writer has lost vitality; this is frequent in the handwriting of people who are nearing the end of their lives.

Of special interest are letters that end in tiny loops or squares at the bottom of the downstroke. This type of lower loop shows a tendency toward sexual frustration or sexual deviation. Tendency toward deviation may remain latent and never be practiced.

Sharp triangles instead of rounded loops are found in the writing of active, persistent people.

A return stroke, curved backward at the bottom of the downstroke, instead of a loop, shows vanity, selfishness; these writers are susceptible to flattery.

A forward stroke at the bottom of the downstroke, instead of a loop, indicates keen perception and impatience.

Omitted lower loops express rapidity of thought and action, and an energetic nature.

UPPER LOOP

1. Low	Low upper loops	Unimaginative, submissive
2. Moderately high	Moderately high	Self-assured, realistic
3. Very high	Very high	Vain, imaginative, eccentric, fanatic
4. Around stem	d, d, t, t	Sensitive, critical
5. Omitted	b, f, h, k	Keen, responsive, active, impatient

LOWER LOOP

1. Short	g y z p	Feeble, passive
2. Medium	g y z p	Submissive, compliant
3. Long		Sportive, restless, active
4. Extremely long	y g z p	Disorganized, unstable, confused

5. Full, inflated		Materialistic, active, sensuous
6. Quavery		Fatigued, weak, passive, ailing
7. Tiny, bottom		Sexually frustrated, deviated
8. Triangular		Persistent, active, impatient
9. Backward stroke, no loop		Clannish, critical, selfish
10. Down, forward to right, no loop		Initiatory, perceptive, impatient
11. Omitted		Decisive, keen, energetic, speedy

■

Seventy-two-year-old cancer patient, Puerto Rico Veterans' Hospital.

The tremulous writing of this man, afflicted with cancer of the cheek and lips, and the pen pressure, fading out almost completely in the upper loops of the letter "f" (fume) and "h" (ha) indicate his generally weakened condition and some physical or mental disorder. It is interesting to note that weakness appears in the same zone of his writing (the upper zone) as does his affliction in his body (upper part).

Carlos Ortiz, world lightweight boxing champion.

Rapid thought and fast action are two traits of this boxing champ, which can be seen in the pointed, angular letters "m" and "n" in his handwriting. The relatively, long "t" crosses starting with heavy pen pressure, some of which are set low on the stems, indicate a desire for quick results, as well as determination. The long upper loops, plus the inflated lower loop in the letter "z" of his signature, portray a vivid imagination and a love of activity. His emotional, responsive nature is evident in the forward slant of his handwriting.

Chapter 7

SMALL, KNOTTED LOOPS

The tiny additional loop (formed like a little knot inserted in a letter) expresses more detailed attitudes and peculiarities often concealed from others.

Upper Zone

Middle Zone — three zones

Lower Zone

A small loop that is formed around the upper stem of a letter shows imagination, persistence, and a literary bent.

An inserted small loop in the middle zone of a letter is indicative of a secretive, persistent, and critical nature.

A writer who inserts several small loops in a single letter, frequently seen in the letters "a", "o", "g", "y", is evasive, and his reasoning is distorted.

If a tiny loop is formed around the lower stem of a letter, it is expressive of eccentricity, mental or physical debility, or sexual frustration or deviation.

Inserted tiny, additional loops in letters, in any of the three zones, always indicate some kind of persistency.

Illustrations follow:

SMALL, KNOTTED LOOP

1. Around upper zone, stem		Persistent, critical, imaginative, literary
2. Middle zone		Persistent, secretive, critical
3. Double-looped, middle zone		Evasive, reasoning distorted
4. Around lower stem		Sexually frustrated, deviating

Take caution in passing judgment on unfavorable traits. Handwriting reveals character tendencies, but they may not always be practiced.

■

Deseo el mejor de los éxitos a esta "charming" señorita. Que su trabajo le produzca la mayor felicidad a ella y a muchas otras personas.

Hiram Cancio

The Hon. Hiram Cancio, Secretary of Justice for the Commonwealth of Puerto Rico.

The evenly-spaced lines and words in the handwriting of this well-liked administrator and judge show that he has excellent sense of timing and sound reasoning. His capacity to concentrate, and the thoroughness with which he thinks and acts, is apparent in the "i" dots that are never omitted. And the small, knotted loop of the letter "H" in the signature is a mark of persistence.

Chapter 8

CAPITAL AND SMALL LETTERS

Capital letters are the thermometer of the ego. When they are moderately high in proportion to the small letters, they indicate a reasonable amount of ego: pride, self-respect, and self-assurance.

Capital letters that are extremely high express much ego: pride, vanity, and perhaps pretense. Extremely high capitals, followed by tiny letters, show that the writer has good intelligence, excessive pride, is self-assured, critical, and quite likely absorbed in himself.

Low capitals indicate modesty, and an unassuming nature. Very low capitals mean the ego has gone down to nearly zero and express an introverted writer, who lacks confidence and may be indifferent toward others.

There are other aspects of capital formation besides their relative height which should be noted. Very ornate capital letters indicate a person given to pomposity and pretentious display. The reverse holds true for a person who makes simple capital letters; he will shun display, be more direct and factual.

Printed capitals (as well as printed small letters) in a predominantly longhand writing express good mental development, originality, and often creative, artistic inclinations.

Many people take pains with the formation of capital letters, since these start sentences, names, and titles, but few people pay much attention to the way they write small letters. And it is precisely because they are written unconsciously that they are so revealing.

This quality of small letters is particularly utilized by handwriting experts in forgery detections. A forger will nearly always exercise great care in copying the capital letters of a signature; but he will take relatively little pains with those important small letters. Hence, the small letters are often the key to solutions of forgery cases.

Small letters that are very large compared with capital letters demonstrate either unjustified pride, little intelligence, or immaturity. These enlarged small letters are noticeable in the writing of children.

CAPITAL LETTERS

1. Capital letters, moderately high	Capital moderate	Confident, realistic
2. Capital letters, extremely high	Capital high	Conceited, self-assured
3. Capital letters, low	Capital low	Modest, unassuming
4. Capital letters, very low	capital very low	Introverted, indifferent
5. Capital letters, printed, unique	Capital Printed	Perceptive, original

SMALL LETTERS

1. Small letters, extremely small	small, small letters extremely small	Intelligent, reserved reserved

2. Small letters, enlarged	Enlarged	Immature, illusive
3. Small letters, "e", "r"	Enlarged	Conceited, selfish

J'ai toujours été très
intéressée par votre art.
Il est plus facile
de maquiller son visage ou sa
personnalité que son écriture.
Que pensez-vous de la mienne?
Bravo — Musicalement
votre Vicky Autier

Vicky Autier, French pianist-singer.

Vicky, a popular pianist-singer "discovered" by the Duchess of Windsor, expresses great originality and imagination in the unique formation of her capital letters, as well as in the disconnected letters within words. The letter "r", written with a square top, is a particularly interesting feature of her writing. This type of "r" indicates both strong will power and dexterity with her hands, so valuable for a versatile pianist.

The canvas is now complete, and as the painter pauses to sit back and admire his freshly painted portrait, you too are entitled to a congratulatory moment of repose.

Having grasped the significance of the elements of handwriting, you are now aware of what signs to isolate and scrutinize in any script you may wish to study.

Handwriting is so complex an activity that no one could recall all the possible meaningful variations of style after a simple reading of this volume. Put the book beside you as you analyze a handwriting sample. Check the meanings of each style quirk with the corresponding chapter in the book. You will find that, after a time, you are able to recall a steadily growing number of basic and individual feature meanings, without having always to look them up.

As your memory for handwriting signs increases, so will the speed and ease with which you can complete an analysis.

The remaining pages of this book are devoted to an Instant Aptitude Guide listing many character traits and abilities. Signs of possible health deficiencies, as well as unfavorable character traits, can also be found there. Your having read carefully through Parts I and II has already given you much of the information—in a different form—that the following Guide presents.

Although it is prepared especially to give a speedy sketch of character and ability, you can use the Guide either for its express purpose or as a means of reviewing what you have learned in the foregoing pages.

The portrait painter may, while taking his ease, dabble in the paints on his palette. And you, in respite from all the learning of Parts I and II, may want to do the same. The Instant Aptitude Guide is an intriguing dabbling place.

PART III

INSTANT CHARACTER AND APTITUDE GUIDE

with

Health and Character

Warning Signs

A pastel-sketched portrait is often done rapidly, capturing in brief strokes several distinct features of a face. This Guide gives you the equivalent of a pastel sketch. With its aid, you will see in an instant distinct aptitudes, character weaknesses, or even signs of latent illness.

DO YOU KNOW . . .

if you are doing the work for which you are really suited?

with what talents teen-age children are gifted, which might be developed through the right course of education?

which is the right person for that special position in your organization?

This Aptitude Guide will enable you to answer all these questions faster than any other method. Find, in the index that follows, the type of work in which you are interested. Then place the handwriting beside the page. If many of the signs in the Aptitude Guide are present in the handwriting, you can be certain that the writer is qualified for that type of work.

INSTANT CHARACTER AND APTITUDE GUIDE

A. LAWYER, POLITICIAN

CONNECTED LETTERS seven or more *within a word* Thorough reasoning, Eloquence	INITIAL STROKES frequently omitted Self-reliance, Rapidity of thought	FINAL STROKES down, forward to right Initiative, Speedy action	"T" CROSSES firm, long Perseverance, Determination
INVERTED "n" LIKE "v" Keen psychological insight	DIMINISHING WORDS slightly *tapering* Diplomacy, Shrewdness	SMALL, KNOTTED LOOPS <u>middle zone</u> Perseverance, Discretion	LETTERS "g", "y", LIKE 9, 7 Calculative ability, Quick perception
LETTERS "o", "a", "d", "g" mostly closed Discretion, Diplomacy	ANGULAR WRITING Firmness, Perception, Aggressiveness	SPACING between lines, words *Even* Consistency, Good reasoning power	LETTERS IN UPPER ZONE moderately high Self-confidence, Realism
EXTENDED WRITING *spread out* Spontaneity, Enterprise	UPPER AND LOWER LOOPS frequently omitted Rapidity of thought and action	GREEK LETTERS "e", "d" Literary inclination, Intelligence	BASE LINE fairly straight *level* Dependability, Good judgment

These signs gauge the person's ability. The more there are, the greater the ability.

B. EXECUTIVE, ORGANIZER, MANAGER

SLANT vertical, a bit forward almost vertical Controlled emotions, Reasoning power	CROSS STROKES firm, long, high T t f TT Long-range planning, Keen imagination	PEN PRESSURE fairly heavy medium - heavy Spontaneity, Determination	ANGULAR WRITING m g h Firmness, Perception, Aggressiveness
PRINTED LETTERS among longhand writing A E K L T Versatility, Individual ideas	CONNECTED, DISCONNECTED LETTERS within words combination Eloquence, Reasoning, Versatility, Imagination	INVERTED "n" LIKE "v" Keen psychological insight	DIMINISHING WORDS slightly Tapering Diplomacy, Shrewdness
UPPER AND LOWER LOOPS frequently omitted b h y z Rapidity of thought and action	FINAL STROKES down, forward to right Initiative, Speedy action	SMALL, KNOTTED LOOPS <u>middle zone</u> Perseverance, Discretion	BASE LINE fairly straight level Dependability, Good judgment
SPACING between lines, words Even Consistency, Good reasoning power	LETTERS IN UPPER ZONE moderately high a C k t Self-confidence, Realism	EXTENDED WRITING spread out Spontaneity, Enterprise	LETTERS "g", "y" LIKE 9, 7 9 7 Calculative ability, Quick perception

BASE LINE fairly straight *level* Dependability, Good judgment	UPPER AND LOWER LOOPS frequently omitted *b f j h* Rapidity of thought and action	CROSS STROKES high *f t tt* Keen imagination, Premeditation	MARGIN well-proportioned *on all sides* Consistency, Sense of proportion
LETTERS IN UPPER ZONE high *h k l* Discrimination, Aspiration	PRINTED LETTERS among longhand writing E W F K Versatility, Individual ideas	PEN PRESSURE well-shaded *U H s f* Sense of design, Good color sense	ANGULAR WRITING *w f h* Firmness, Perception, Aggressiveness
SMALL, KNOTTED LOOPS middle zone *o g b f* Perseverance, Discretion	CONNECTED, DISCONNECTED LETTERS within words *combination* Eloquence, Reasoning, Versatility, Imagination	"I" DOT right of stem *i i i* Rapidity of thought, Progressive ideas	SPACING between lines, words *Even* Consistency, Good reasoning power
DIMINISHING WORDS slightly *Tapering* Diplomacy, Shrewdness	FINAL STROKES down, forward to right *y g f* Initiative, Speedy action	EXTENDED WRITING *spread out* Spontaneity, Enterprise	LETTERS "g", "y" LIKE 9, 7 *9 7* Calculative ability, Quick perception

The greater the number of these signs in a handwriting, the more suitable the person.

D. ADVERTISER, PROMOTER, PUBLICITY AGENT

GREEK LETTERS "e", "d" Literary inclination, Intelligence	CROSS STROKES high Keen imagination, Premeditation	PRINTED LETTERS among longhand writing A E h T Versatility, Individual ideas	ANGULAR WRITING Firmness, Perception, Aggressiveness
LETTER "T" LIKE "x" Sense of design, Inventiveness	INITIAL STROKES frequently omitted Self-reliance, Rapidity of thought	DIMINISHING WORDS slightly Tapering Diplomacy, Shrewdness	"I" DOTS high, right of stem Progressive ideas, Imagination
ORIGINAL-TYPE LETTERS Creativeness, Originality	CONNECTED, DISCONNECTED LETTERS within words combination Eloquence, Reasoning, Versatility, Imagination	LETTERS IN UPPER ZONE high Aspiration, Discrimination	EXTENDED WRITING spread out Spontaneity, Enterprise
SMALL, KNOTTED LOOPS <u>middle zone</u> Perseverance, Discretion	FINAL STROKES down, forward to right Initiative, Speedy action	SPACING between lines, words Even Consistency, Good reasoning power	"T" CROSSES firm, long Perseverance Determination

BASE LINE slightly upward *upward* Optimism, Ambition	"T" CROSSES long, hooked Aggressiveness, Persistence	DIMINISHING WORDS slightly *tapering* Diplomacy, Shrewdness	LETTERS "g", "y" LIKE 9, 7 9 7 Calculative ability, Quick perception
LOWER LOOPS long Intense drive, Physical vitality	PEN PRESSURE heavy *heavy* Aggressiveness, Spontaneity	"I" DOTS right of stem Progressive ideas, Rapidity of thought	INITIAL STROKES frequently omitted Rapidity of thought, Self-reliance
SLANT slightly forward *forward* Spontaneity, Determination	SMALL, KNOTTED LOOPS middle zone Perseverance, Discretion	CONNECTED, DISCONNECTED LETTERS within words *combination* Eloquence, Reasoning, Versatility, Imagination	INVERTED "n" LIKE "v" Keen psychological insight
ANGULAR WRITING Firmness, Perception, Aggressiveness	EXTENDED WRITING *spread out* Spontaneity, Enterprise	FINAL STROKES down, forward to right Initiative, Speedy action	SPACING between lines, words *Even* Consistency, Good reasoning power

The more combinations of these signs in a handwriting, the better qualified the person.

F. SECRETARY, ACCOUNTANT, DETAIL OR RESEARCH WORKER

ROUNDED AND ANGULAR writing *both* Tact, Friendliness, Alertness	"T" CROSSES even on sides of stem *t t t t* Stability, Precision	SIZE OF WRITING medium-small *fairly small* Concentration, Compliance	U-SHAPED "m", "n" *m n* Adaptability, Diplomacy
LOWER LOOPS medium long *p g f* Compliance, Submissiveness	LEGIBLE WRITING *clear, simple* Accuracy, Constancy	LETTERS "o", "a", "d", "g" closed *o a d g* Discretion, Diplomacy	BASE LINE fairly straight *level* Dependability, Good judgment
SPACING between lines, words *Even* Consistency, Good reasoning power	"I" DOT directly above stem *i i i* Concentration, Precision	CONNECTED LETTERS seven or more *within a word* Thorough reasoning, Eloquence	INITIAL STROKES frequently omitted *a b h t* Rapidity of thought, Self-reliance
LETTERS IN UPPER ZONE moderately high *l m d* Self-confidence, Realism	SLANT vertical, a bit forward *almost vertical* Controlled emotions, Reasoning power		

LETTERS "m", "n", "r" flat, square on top m n r Manual dexterity, Technical proficiency	ORIGINAL-TYPE LETTERS D M U V II Creativeness, Originality	LETTER "T" LIKE "x" + T x Sense of design, Inventiveness	LETTERS "g", "y" LIKE 9, 7 9 7 7 Calculative ability, Quick perception
UPPER AND LOWER LOOPS full, inflated B G S Eccentricity, Ostentation	ANGULAR WRITING m g h Firmness, Perception Aggressiveness	MARGIN well-proportioned on all sides Sense of proportion, Consistency	INITIAL STROKES frequently omitted o b h t Self-reliance, Rapidity of thought
PRINTED LETTERS among longhand writing A E W T Versatility, Individual ideas	SPACING between lines, words Even Good reasoning power, Consistency	LETTERS IN UPPER ZONE high l h N Aspiration, Discrimination	BASE LINE fairly straight level Dependability, Good judgment
CONNECTED, DISCONNECTED LETTERS within words combination Eloquence, Reasoning, Versatility, Imagination	CROSS STROKES high T F))) Keen imagination, Premeditation	EXTENDED WRITING spread out Spontaneity, Enterprise	"T" CROSSES firm, long T t t Perseverance, Determination

These signs gauge the person's ability. The more there are, the greater the ability.

H. DESIGNER, INTERIOR DECORATOR, ARTIST, SCULPTOR

ORIGINAL-TYPE LETTERS W D M Creativeness, Originality	LETTERS "m", "n", "r" flat, square on top m n r Manual dexterity, Technical proficiency	LETTER "T" LIKE "x" Sense of design, Inventiveness	LETTER "g" LIKE NO. 8 Intellect, Cultured tastes
PRINTED LETTERS among longhand writing A E W T Versatility, Individual ideas	MARGIN well-proportioned on all sides Consistency, Sense of proportion	INITIAL STROKES frequently omitted o a b t Self-reliance, Rapidity of thought	LETTERS IN UPPER ZONE high l h N Aspiration, Discrimination
CROSS STROKES high T F Keen imagination, Premeditation	PEN PRESSURE well-shaded L C H Sense of design, Good color sense	CONNECTED, DISCONNECTED LETTERS within words combination Eloquence, Reasoning, Versatility, Imagination	LETTERS "g", "y" LIKE 9, 7 9 7 Calculative ability, Quick perception
SPACING between lines, words even Good reasoning power, Consistency	"I" DOT high, right of stem i i i Progressive ideas, Imagination	UPPER AND LOWER LOOPS full, inflated B G g Eccentricity, Ostentation	EXTENDED WRITING spread out Spontaneity, Enterprise

UPPER AND LOWER LOOPS full, inflated Eccentricity, Ostentation	PRINTED LETTERS among longhand writing A E h T Versatility, Individual ideas	CROSS STROKES wavy Comic, mimic sense, Flamboyance	UPPER AND LOWER LOOPS frequently omitted Rapidity of thought and action
"I" DOT wavy, original Wit, Humor, Originality	CONNECTED, DISCONNECTED LETTERS within words combination Eloquence, Reasoning, Versatility, Imagination	ANGULAR WRITING Firmness, Perception, Aggressiveness	LETTERS LIKE MUSICAL notes or symbols Rhythm, Harmony, Musical imagination
SMALL, KNOTTED LOOPS upper zone Eccentricity, Literary imagination	CROSS STROKES high Keen imagination, Premeditation	EXTENDED WRITING spread out Spontaneity, Enterprise	FINAL DOWNSTROKES spiraled, curled Eccentricity, Evasiveness
FINAL STROKES down, forward to right Initiative, Speedy action	PEN PRESSURE heavy heavy Aggressiveness, Spontaneity	ORIGINAL-TYPE LETTERS Creativeness, Originality	"T" CROSSES firm, long Perseverance, Determination

These signs gauge the person's ability. The more there are, the greater the ability.

J. COMPOSER, CHOREOGRAPHER, CREATIVE WRITER

LETTERS LIKE MUSICAL notes or symbols Rhythm, Harmony, Musical imagination	SMALL, KNOTTED LOOPS upper zone Eccentricity, Literary imagination	CROSS STROKES high Keen imagination, Premeditation	GREEK LETTERS "e", "d" Literary inclination, Intelligence
LETTER "g" LIKE NO. 8 Cultured tastes, Intellect	SIZE OF WRITING small small writing Good memory, High intelligence	ORIGINAL-TYPE LETTERS Creativeness, Originality	PRINTED LETTERS among longhand writing A E h T Versatility, Individual ideas
UPPER AND LOWER LOOPS full, inflated Ostentation, Eccentricity	FINAL DOWNSTROKES spiraled, curled Eccentricity, Evasiveness	CONNECTED, DISCONNECTED LETTERS within words combination Eloquence, Reasoning, Versatility, Imagination	SPACING between lines, words Even Consistency, Good reasoning power
CROSS STROKES high Comic, mimic sense, Flamboyance	"I" DOT wavy, original Wit, Humor, Originality	"T" CROSSES long, firm Perseverance, Determination	BASE LINE fairly straight fairly Dependability, Good judgment

GREEK LETTERS "e", "d" ε ∂ ε ∂ Literary inclination, Intelligence	LETTER "T" LIKE "x" Sense of design, Inventiveness	SIZE OF WRITING small small writing High intelligence, Good memory	LETTER "g" LIKE NO. 8 Intellect, Cultured tastes
CONNECTED LETTERS seven or more within a word Thorough reasoning, Eloquence	LETTERS "g", "y" LIKE 9, 7 9 7 7 Calculative ability, Quick perception	PRINTED LETTERS among longhand writing A E h T Versatility, Individual ideas	MARGIN well-proportioned on all sides Consistency, Sense of proportion
"I" DOT directly above stem i i i Concentration, Precision	SPACING between lines, words even Consistency, Good reasoning power	SMALL, KNOTTED LOOPS middle zone o a b f Perseverance, Discretion	ANGULAR WRITING m g h Firmness, Perception, Aggressiveness
BASE LINE fairly straight level Dependability, Good judgment	LETTERS IN UPPER ZONE high l h h Aspiration, Discrimination	SLANT vertical, a bit forward almost vertical Controlled emotions, Reasoning power	"T" CROSSES even on sides of stem t t t t Stability, Precision

The more combinations of these signs in a handwriting, the better qualified the person.

L. PHYSICIAN, SURGEON, DENTIST, PSYCHOLOGIST

INVERTED "n" LIKE "v" n v Keen psychological insight	FINAL STROKES long, rounded o a s d Humanity, Charity	INITIAL STROKES frequently omitted o b h t Self-reliance, Rapidity of thought	"T" CROSSES firm, long t t t Perseverance, Determination
LETTERS "a", "o", "d", "g" mostly closed a o d g Discretion, Diplomacy	CONNECTED LETTERS seven or more within a word Thorough reasoning, Eloquence	ANGULAR WRITING m g h Firmness, Perception, Aggressiveness	GREEK LETTERS "e", "d" ε ∂ ε ∂ Literary inclination, Intelligence
LETTERS "g", "y" LIKE 9, 7 9 7 Calculative ability, Quick perception	U-SHAPED "m", "n" m n Diplomacy, Adaptability	BASE LINE fairly straight level Dependability, Good judgment	LETTERS "m", "n", "r" flat, square on top m n r Technical proficiency, Manual dexterity
"I" DOTS above stem i i i Concentration, Precision	SPACING between lines, words even Consistency, Good reasoning power	LETTER "g" LIKE NO. 8 8 8 8 Intellect, Cultured tastes	SLANT vertical, a bit forward almost vertical Controlled emotions, Reasoning power

The more combinations of these signs in a handwriting, the better qualified the person.

<table>
<tr>
<td>FINAL STROKES
long, rounded
o a s d
Humanity,
Charity</td>
<td>ROUNDED AND ANGULAR
writing
both
Tact, Friendliness,
Alertness</td>
<td>"T" CROSSES
low
t t t
Sympathy,
Prompt action</td>
<td>SLANT
vertical, a bit forward
almost vertical
Controlled emotions,
Reasoning power</td>
</tr>
<tr>
<td>LETTERS "m", "n", "r"
flat, square on top
m n r
Technical proficiency,
Manual dexterity</td>
<td>LOWER LOOPS
medium long
f g p
Submissiveness,
Compliance</td>
<td>SPACING
between lines, words
even
Consistency,
Good reasoning power</td>
<td>U-SHAPED "m", "n"
u u
Adaptability,
Diplomacy</td>
</tr>
<tr>
<td>"I" DOTS
directly above stem
i i i
Concentration,
Precision</td>
<td>CONNECTED LETTERS
seven or more
within a word
Thorough reasoning,
Eloquence</td>
<td>INVERTED "n" LIKE "v"
v v v
Keen psychological
insight</td>
<td>LEGIBLE WRITING
clear, simple
Accuracy,
Constancy</td>
</tr>
<tr>
<td>BASE LINE
fairly straight
level
Dependability,
Good judgment</td>
<td>LETTERS "o", "a", "d",
"g" mostly closed
o a d g
Discretion,
Diplomacy</td>
<td>SIZE OF WRITING
fairly small
medium - small
Concentration,
Good memory</td>
<td>INITIAL STROKES
frequently omitted
a w b k
Rapidity of thought,
Self-reliance</td>
</tr>
</table>

The greater the number of these signs in a handwriting, the more suitable the person.

N. ATHLETE, PHYSICAL EDUCATION INSTRUCTOR

LETTER "P" long-looped, <u>lower zone</u> p p p Sportmanship, Athletic interest	"T" CROSSES heavy, firm, long t t t Endurance, Confidence Determination	LOWER LOOPS long g f f z Intense drive, Physical vitality	SLANT slightly forward forward Spontaneity, Determination
ANGULAR WRITING m w g h Firmness, Perception, Aggressiveness	PEN PRESSURE heavy heavy Aggressiveness, Spontaneity	SMALL, KNOTTED LOOPS <u>middle zone</u> o f tt t Perseverance, Discretion	"I" DOTS above or right of stem i i i Foresight, Rapidity of thought
INITIAL STROKES frequently omited o m b h Rapidity of thought, Self-reliance	FINAL STROKES down, forward to right Initiative, Speedy action	SPACING between lines, words Even Consistency, Good reasoning power	INVERTED "n" LIKE "v" Keen psychological insight
MARGIN well-proportioned on all sides Sense of proportion and design			

The greater the number of these signs in a handwriting, the more suitable the person.

HEALTH AND CHARACTER WARNING SIGNS

DO YOU KNOW . . .

that physical or mental problems can be spotted in the signs of a person's handwriting?

that certain signs in a handwriting can warn you of a person who is insincere, untrustworthy, or even dangerous?

Compare the writing sample you have with the illustrations on the following two tables to see if the writer shows signs of actual or latent illness or unfavorable traits.

Remember, however, two important precautions:

1. Illness signs, although significant, should not substitute for a doctor's diagnosis. If signs in the script lead you to conclude that illness is present, you should not take the responsibility of declaring that the writer is suffering from a specific ailment. The writing signs serve only as a hint, which should be followed by a full medical diagnosis.

2. Do not jump to conclusions about unfavorable signs. Do not judge a person totally insincere, for example, because of a few insincerity signs in his handwriting. An occasional insincerity sign in an otherwise sincere script means that the writer is basically honest, but he may in some minor matters not be so scrupulous. If, however, the writer always shows insincerity in the parts of his script that gauge this trait, he is basically insincere.

Most people are mixtures of what we call good and bad traits. No person is entirely without virtue, nor is any person so free of faults that he can be considered perfect. The saints are all in heaven.

Some have traits that most people consider dangerous in certain situations. It can be of vital importance to you to determine just how consistently one of these traits is present in a person's nature.

It is always the relative frequency of an unfavorable or dangerous sign in the sample that will give you this information. That is why it is so important to obtain as long a sample of handwriting as possible for an accurate analysis.

O. PHYSICAL OR MENTALL ILLNESS—ACTUAL OR LATENT

WRITING extremely ornamental *Fantasy* Mental confusion, Extravagant fancy	STROKES beadlike dots *o d m g* Symptoms of physical disease	PEN PRESSURE heavy <u>up</u>strokes *t M h* Symptoms of physical disease	PEN PRESSURE extremely thin *no stamina* Physical or mental weakness
SLANT extremely changeable *unpredictable* Inconsistency, Emotional instability	LETTERS deteriorated, shaky *g p f h* Physical weakness, Unbalanced mind	SMALL, KNOTTED LOOPS around <u>lower stem</u> *g [illegible] z [illegible]* Sexual frustration or deviation	UPPER, LOWER LOOPS tangle in other lines *Confusion* Confusion, Neurosis, Emotional instability
STENCIL WRITING feather- edged *feather-edge* Mental derangement, Alcohol, drug addiction	LETTERS indented, curved-in Physical ailment, Localized malfunction	STROKES blurry, dim spots *a k [illegible]* Physical deficiency, Malfunction	
WRITING heavy, muddy, smeary *Mental disturbance* Uncontrolled emotion, Drug, alcohol addiction	LOWER LOOPS short, thin pen pressures *y g p y* Loss of energy and stamina	SLANT extremely downward *Depression* Depression, Despondency, Despair	

Recommend qualified medical assistance if these signs appear frequently in a handwriting.

P. UNFAVORABLE OR DANGEROUS TRAITS

RETRACED LETTERS added loops, strokes Insincerity, Concealment	INITIAL STROKES sliced "a", "o", "d", "g" Cunning, Dishonesty	"T" CROSSES clublike finals Uncontrolled temper, Violence, Brutality	SIGNATURE encircled, crossed-out Concealment, Cunning Misrepresentation
FINAL STROKES downward, to right Obstinacy, Short temper	LETTERS "a", "o", "d", "g" open at bottom Deceit, Fraudulence, Criminal tendency	DOUBLE-KNOTTED LOOPS in middle zone Evasion, Distorted reasoning	"T" CROSSES heavy starting point Sudden temper, Impulsiveness
SLANT extremely changeable unpredictable Inconsistency, Instability	LETTERS "e", "a", "o", "d", "g" clogged with ink Sex mania, Uncontrolled emotions	WRITING heavy, muddy, smeary Mental disturbance Violence, Brutality, Drug, alcohol addiction	SLANT extremely downward Depression Depression Despondency, Despair
"T" CROSSES bowl-curved Shallow, Drifting, Weak-willed	SMALL, KNOTTED LOOPS around lower stem Sexual frustration or deviation	STENCIL WRITING feather-edged feather-edge Mental derangement, Alcohol, drug addiction	BASE LINE extremely wavy unreliability Instability, Inconsistency

Be cautious passing judgment. Only repeated signs establish an accurate analysis.